Kids' Recipes for Success™

A Cookbook By And For Kids

Compiled and Edited by Barbara DeMarco

Illustrations by Bill Kantz.

Table of Contents

Introduction

The makers of Success® Rice had an idea . . . ask children to submit their favorite recipes and craft ideas for inclusion in a cookbook, for and by kids, and call it **Kids' Recipes for Success™.** After all, current studies show American children are spending more time in the kitchen than ever before. Well, with a pinch of this and a taste of that, the idea became a reality and guess what happened?

Children from Lawrence, Kansas; Portland, Oregon; Beaver Falls, Pennsylvania; and literally, every corner of America told us their stories. Stories of learning to bake with grandmothers, helping with dinner on "Mom's night off," and cooking with friends after school.

Stories aside, American children love to experiment and create in the kitchen and the recipes we received proved it — Nut Nana Toast, Raggedy Robins and Apple-Rice Pizza. More than 600 recipes poured in — many more than we had room for!

There's no easy recipe for developing a child's self esteem, but the makers of Success Rice believe that parental involvement and family activities like cooking with children are vital ingredients.

Thanks to all of you who shared your favorite recipes with us. Not only are you continuing a wonderful tradition of kids in the kitchen, but you're making an invaluable contribution to the March of Dimes Campaign for Healthier Babies and its efforts to improve the health of mothers and babies.

What are you waiting for? Put on your apron and enjoy!

The Author

Barbara DeMarco

As a professional dietitian, Barbara DeMarco plays a key role in product and recipe development for all of Riviana Foods' products — including Success® Rice. More than just mixing ingredients, Barbara focuses much of her attention on food chemistry and nutrition.

Barbara has taught at The University of Houston's Department of Human Development and Consumer Sciences and at the Conrad Hilton School of Hotel and Restaurant Management.

A graduate of Texas Women's University with a master's degree in nutrition, Barbara is a member of the American Dietetic Association and the American and Houston Home Economics Associations.

Barbara has been married for eight years and is the mother of five-year-old twins who love to help her in the kitchen.

Kid Panelists

"Yummy!" "Yucky!" "May I have seconds?" These were just a few of the responses we heard from our expert panel of kid judges as they helped select the final recipes for the **Kids' Recipes for Success™** cookbook. Twelve judges meant 12 cooks in the kitchen, and cook they did — Peanut Butter Bars & Frosting, Grandmother's Porcupine Balls, Rice Cheddar Melts and lots more! Some tough decisions were made but all of the judges agreed — kids love to cook **and** sample the successful recipes!

A big chef's hat off to our expert panel of kid judges:

- Ose Edbor, Age 12
- Minnie DuPlantis, Age 10
- Lindsay Calvert, Age 7
- Josh Palmer, Age 10
- Nick DuPlantis, Age 13
- Brittany McClure, Age 11
- Megan Coody, Age 8
- Evan Calvert, Age 9
- Nosa Edebor, Age 8
- Aaron Smith, Age 8
- Kelly Squire, Age 9
- Shannon Squire, Age 7

From the March of Dimes Birth Defects Foundation

For more than 50 years, the March of Dimes has worked to make kids healthier. First, we found out how to stop a terrible disease, polio, from hurting children. Now, we're working to help babies be born healthy.

Our Campaign for Healthier Babies helps by:

- Researching reasons why babies are born sick.
- Funding programs that improve the health of mothers and babies.
- Convincing community leaders that the health of mothers and babies is very important.
- Teaching everybody about how to improve their chances of having a healthy baby.

When you buy a copy of **Kids' Recipes for Success™** cookbook, $1 goes to the March of Dimes. Thanks, Success® Rice! And thank you, too, for helping the March of Dimes in its Campaign for Healthier Babies.

Jennifer L. Howse, Ph. D.
President
March of Dimes Birth Defects Foundation

Tips For Getting Started

- **GET ADULT HELP.** Your helper can review the recipe steps with you, answer any questions and help with kitchen tools and hot pans.
- Roll up your sleeves.
- Be sure to wear an apron so clothes stay clean.
- If you have long hair, pull it back so it won't get into the food.
- Wash your hands with soap and water and dry them well.
- Read the recipe all the way through and collect everything you need to prepare the recipe (equipment and ingredients).

Cooking Safety Tips

- Make sure an **adult helper** is around when you're using the oven, range, a sharp knife or electric appliances.
- Always use oven mitts to handle anything hot and make sure they're dry. Use these whenever you take anything out of the oven or microwave.
- When cooking on top of the range, turn the pan handle to the middle of the range. This will prevent anyone from accidentally bumping a hot pan and turning it over.
- When removing a lid from a hot pan or baking dish, be sure to stand back so you're not burned as steam is let out.
- Turn oven and range top dials to "off" as soon as you've finished cooking.
- Range tops take a few minutes to cool down — be careful not to touch the burners.
- Always keep paper towels nearby to wipe up any spills. Clean up anything that spills on the floor right away, so no one slips and falls.

Hints For Clean Up

- Clean up as you go so that it will be easier at the end. (You'll also keep your work space clear of clutter.)

- Put ingredients away as you finish with them, especially cold foods (such as margarine or milk) that belong in the refrigerator. Be sure to replace lids tightly!

- Rinse dishes before food dries on them. Rinse as soon as you're finished with a dish or piece of cooking equipment.

- Wash, dry and put away all the equipment when you're finished cooking. Start by washing the least soiled items first and finish with your messiest pots and pans.

- Be sure and wipe off counters and tables so your mom and dad will want you to cook again.

How To Measure Correctly

Measuring cups for liquids have pouring spouts, to make it easy to pour the liquid out of the measuring cup without spilling. These cups have lines to mark measurements. Place measuring cup on a flat surface. Bend down to look at lines on the cup. Add the liquid slowly until it reaches the mark you want. You will need this cup to measure liquids such as water, milk and honey.

Single metal or plastic cups are used to measure dry ingredients. Carefully scoop flour, sugar, or any other dry ingredient into the dry measuring cup. BE CAREFUL NOT TO SHAKE THE CUP. Pile the dry ingredient high in the cup and level off with a table knife. Never dip the measuring cup into the flour because this will pack any dry ingredient.

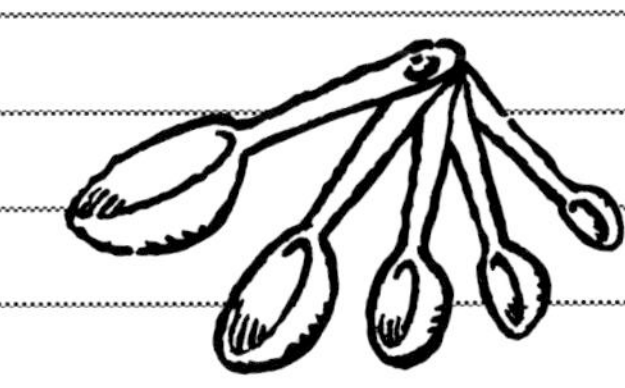

Measuring spoons are metal or plastic. Use the same set of measuring spoons for **both** liquid and dry ingredients. Do not measure with a spoon that you will use at the table. For dry ingredients, be sure to level off with a knife. For liquids, fill the spoon to the top.

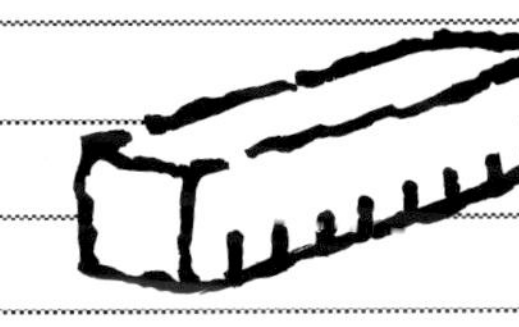

Look closely at the margarine wrapper. Measurements are marked on the wrapper. Using a table knife, cut the amount of margarine needed. One-half cup margarine equals 1 stick of margarine. If you need one-fourth cup or one-third cup, it will be marked on the wrapper.

Rice Facts

- Rice is mankind's largest food crop. People all over the world eat rice. In the United States, we each eat about 18 pounds of rice per year.

- Rice grows once a year. Most of the rice grown in the U.S. is found in six states: Texas, Arkansas, Louisiana, Mississippi, Missouri and California.

- There are three basic types of rice. **Long grain rice** is at least four times as long as it is wide. **Medium grain rice** is plump in shape and **short grain rice** is almost round.

- One of the most nutritious foods available today, rice is low in calories and fat, and, it provides you with lots of energy.

- Riviana Foods Inc., the creator of the **Kids' Recipes for Success™** cookbook, is headquartered in Houston, Texas and is the world's leading marketer of rice products. The company sells rice in the United States and overseas under the following brands: **Success**®, **Carolina**®, **River**®, **Mahatma**® and **Water Maid**®. Next time you're at the store, pick up one of these products — they'll soon become your favorite!

Breakfast

Pancake Sandwiches

By Adam Zucker   Ardsley, New York

Ingredients	Equipment
1/4 medium-size banana, peeled	measuring spoons
2 teaspoons peanut butter	butter knife
2 frozen pancakes, thawed	knife
6 miniature marshmallows	cutting board
6 chocolate chips	paper plate

Slice banana with knife into 1/8-inch thick slices on cutting board. Spread 1 teaspoon peanut butter on each pancake. Place sliced bananas, marshmallows and chocolate chips on top of peanut butter on 1 pancake. Next, place other pancake, peanut butter side down, on top of first pancake and press down gently. Put on paper plate.

Microwave on high for 1 minute or until chocolate chips and marshmallows are melted. Carefully remove plate from microwave. Serve warm.

Apple Spice Muffins

Mary Elizabeth Malinovsky **The Woodlands, Texas**

Ingredients

2 apples
1 1/4 cups flour
1 cup sugar
1/2 teaspoon salt
1 teaspoon baking soda
1 teaspoon apple pie spice
1/4 cup vegetable oil
1 large egg

Equipment

large mixing bowl
small mixing bowl
measuring cups
measuring spoons
knife
cutting board
mixing spoon
rubber spatula
electric mixer
12-cup muffin pan
12 cupcake papers
wire cooling rack
oven mitts
peeler

Preheat oven to 350 degrees.

Peel and core apples. Cut apples into 1/4-inch-sized cubes on the cutting board. Set aside.

Combine flour, sugar, salt, baking soda and apple pie spice in large bowl. Add apples, oil and egg. Beat with electric mixer on medium speed for 1 minute. Pour into muffin pan cups lined with cupcake papers and fill about

2/3 full. Sprinkle top of each muffin with 1/2 teaspoon muffin topping mix — see recipe below.

Bake muffins at 350 degrees for 20 minutes or until toothpick inserted into center of a muffin comes out clean. Carefully remove pan from oven using oven mitts and place on cooling rack. Let cool 10 minutes. Holding muffin pan with oven mitts, turn pan over so muffins fall out on counter top. Place muffins right-side up and finish cooling another 10 minutes. Serve warm. Store leftover muffins in an airtight container.

Muffin Topping

1/2 cup brown sugar
1/4 teaspoon cinnamon

In small bowl, mix sugar and cinnamon together. Set aside until ready to top muffins.

SERVINGS
2

Rice Bee-Nana

Amber Terrones   Pueblo, Colorado

Ingredients	**Equipment**
1 bag Success® Rice	fork
1 banana, peeled	measuring spoons
1 tablespoon honey	small mixing bowl
	microwave-proof dish or 10-inch non-stick frying pan
	mixing spoon, oven mitts

Cook rice according to package instructions. In bowl, mash peeled banana with fork and stir in honey. Add cooked rice to bowl and stir.

To cook in microwave: pour mixture into microwave-proof dish and heat on high 1-2 minutes. Carefully remove dish from microwave with oven mitts.

To cook on top of range: pour mixture into frying pan and put on range burner. Heat on medium setting, stirring with spoon occasionally until hot — about 2-3 minutes.

To serve: Divide mixture between 2 serving dishes and serve warm.

Toad in a Hole

Todd Dwyer   Lawrence, Kansas

Ingredients	**Equipment**
1 slice of bread	8-inch frying pan
1 teaspoon margarine	spatula
1 large egg	biscuit cutter

Using biscuit cutter, cut a 3-inch hole (or a hole big enough to hold an egg) in the middle of bread slice. Place frying pan on range burner and turn to medium heat. Place margarine in pan to melt. Once margarine bubbles, place bread in frying pan. Immediately crack egg into hole and cook until bread begins to turn brown — about 1½ minutes. Turn over with spatula and brown on other side for another 1½ minutes. Remove from frying pan with spatula and serve hot.

Eggs and Rice Dish

Amy Pastor   Crowley, Louisiana

Ingredients

1 bag Success® Rice
½ cup chopped green onions
6 large eggs
1 teaspoon water
2 tablespoons margarine
¼ cup chopped pimientos (optional)
¼ teaspoon salt
⅛ teaspoon pepper

Equipment

cutting board
knife
10-inch frying pan
spatula
medium mixing bowl
fork
measuring cups
measuring spoons

Cook rice according to package directions.

Chop green onions on cutting board. Set aside.

Crack eggs into bowl and add water. Beat with fork (about 1 minute).

Heat frying pan on medium heat, add margarine. When margarine bubbles, add eggs. Next, add green onions, rice, pimientos, salt and pepper. Stir mixture slowly in pan with spatula. Stir every 10 seconds until eggs begin to cook.

Eggs are done after about 2 minutes. **Do not overcook** or eggs will be dry. With spatula, break egg mixture into small chunks. Serve hot.

Nut-Nana Toast

Katie Manassero Oceanside, California

Ingredients
1 English muffin, halved
1 tablespoon peanut butter
1 banana
1 tablespoon wheat germ (optional)
1 tablespoon raisins

Equipment
electric toaster
butter knife
measuring spoons
cutting board

Toast muffin in electric toaster. Spread inside of each toasted muffin half with ½ tablespoon peanut butter.

Slice banana with knife on cutting board into ⅛-inch thick slices. Lay banana slices over peanut butter and sprinkle with wheat germ. Next, sprinkle muffin halves with raisins. Serve warm.

Brunch Strata Breakfast

Jessica N. Elliot   Bedford, Pennsylvania

Ingredients	**Equipment**
Non-stick vegetable spray	knife
12 slices white bread	cutting board
1 cup onion, chopped	9" x 13" x 2" baking pan
2 cups ham cubes	medium mixing bowl
2 cups Swiss cheese, shredded	measuring spoons
8 large eggs	fork
4 cups milk	wire cooling rack
1 teaspoon salt	oven mitts
¼ teaspoon pepper	

Preheat oven to 350 degrees. Spray baking pan with non-stick vegetable spray. Set aside. Using knife and cutting board, cut bread slices into ½-inch cubes. Chop onions and cut ham into ½-inch cubes.

Place bread cubes in an even layer in pan. On top of bread cubes sprinkle a layer each of onion, ham and shredded cheese. Crack eggs into bowl and beat with fork. Add milk, salt and pepper. Pour egg/milk mixture in baking pan.

Bake at 350 degrees for 35 minutes. Carefully remove pan from oven with oven mitts and place on cooling rack. Cool 5 minutes before cutting. Serve hot.

Breakfast Pizza

Emily Matthews   Minnetonka, Minnesota

Ingredients	**Equipment**
1 whole wheat English muffin, halved	cookie sheet
4 teaspoons margarine, softened	butter knife
¼ cup fruit jam	oven mitts
½ cup shredded Mozzarella cheese	wire cooling rack

Preheat oven on broiler setting.

Lightly spread inside of each muffin half with 2 teaspoons margarine and put buttered-side up on cookie sheet.

Place cookie sheet in preheated oven on top oven rack under broiler for about 1 minute or until light brown. Carefully remove cookie sheet from oven using oven mitts and place on cooling rack. Spread each toasted muffin half with half the jam and half the shredded cheese. Place under broiler again until cheese is melted.

Power Smoothy

Katie Manassero   Oceanside, California

Ingredients

1 medium-size banana
1 orange
½ cup of **one** of the following: milk, orange juice, pineapple juice or apple juice
1 cup vanilla yogurt
3-6 ice cubes

Equipment

electric blender
measuring cups
3 (8-ounce) drinking glasses
6 Popsicle® molds (optional)

For best results, chill all ingredients first. Peel banana and cut into 4 pieces. Next, peel and section orange into 4 pieces. Put banana and orange pieces in blender. Add your choice of milk or juice. Add yogurt, cover and blend on high until smooth — about 1 minute. Add 3 ice cubes, 1 at a time, and blend on high until mixture is thick — about 2 minutes. Add remaining ice cubes, if a colder and frostier smoothy is desired. Pour into glasses and serve.

Menu suggestion: Mixture also can be poured into Popsicle® molds and put in freezer until set — about 2 hours.

Bacon 'N Eggs the Easy Way

Mike Slatton Claremore, Oklahoma

Ingredients	**Equipment**
1 large egg	small mixing bowl
1 tablespoon bacon bits	fork
1 tablespoon Cheddar cheese, grated	measuring spoons
¼ teaspoon water	spatula
Pinch of salt and pepper	small frying pan
1 teaspoon margarine	

Crack egg into bowl and beat with fork. Add bacon bits, cheese, water, salt and pepper. Beat with fork to blend.

Put frying pan on range burner and turn heat to medium. Add margarine. When margarine bubbles, add egg mixture. Let stand about 10 seconds. Stir mixture slowly with spatula. Stir every 10 seconds until egg begins to cook. Egg will be done after about 2 minutes. **Do not overcook** or egg will be dry. With spatula, break egg mixture into bite-size chunks. Serve hot.

Farm Pancake Puff

Crystal Brookes Gales Creek, Oregon

Ingredients

Non-stick vegetable oil spray
3 large eggs
1½ cups milk
¼ cup cottage cheese
1 tablespoon sugar
¾ cup all-purpose flour

For Garnish:

Fresh fruit, sour cream or warm maple syrup and powdered sugar

Equipment

9-inch metal pie plate
food processor or blender
small mixing bowl
mixing spoon
oven mitts
measuring cups
measuring spoons
knife

Spray pie plate with non-stick spray. Set aside.

Preheat oven to 425 degrees.

Add eggs, milk and cottage cheese to work bowl of food processor or blender. In mixing bowl, blend sugar and flour together. Turn on processor or blender at low speed to combine ingredients — for 1 minute. Then add flour/sugar mixture. Blend until ingredients are mixed — about 1 minute.

Put oiled pie plate in preheated oven for 2 minutes to heat. With oven mitts, remove from oven carefully and pour prepared batter into pie plate. Carefully put filled pie plate in oven.

Bake at 425 degrees for 15 minutes or until batter is firm and pancake is high and puffy. With oven mitts, remove carefully from oven and let cool on wire rack 2-3 minutes before cutting into 4 portions. Serve pancake warm and top with your favorite fresh fruit and sour cream or warm maple syrup or powdered sugar.

Rice Pancakes

Jessica Madelyn Matarese **Burlington, New Jersey**

Ingredients	**Equipment**
1 bag Success® Rice	8-inch frying pan
2 large eggs	spatula
Pinch of salt and pepper	fork
1 tablespoon margarine	large spoon
Pancake syrup (to taste)	medium mixing bowl
Margarine (to taste)	

Cook rice according to package directions.

Crack eggs into bowl. Slightly beat eggs with fork. Add cooked rice, salt and pepper and mix. Turn range burner to medium heat and lightly grease frying pan with margarine. Place pan on burner and when hot, drop mixture by spoonfuls into pan. Brown 2 minutes on each side, turning with spatula.

Serve hot with margarine and pancake syrup.

Rice Breakfast Cereal

Jesse Ogden   Tigard, Oregon

PREP TIME
15 min.

SERVINGS
4

Ingredients
1 bag Success Rice®
2 cups milk or cream
1 teaspoon margarine
1/2 teaspoon nutmeg
1/8 teaspoon ground cloves
1 teaspoon cinnamon

Equipment
saucepan
measuring cups
measuring spoons
mixing spoon

Cook rice according to package directions.

Put saucepan on range burner and add cooked rice, milk or cream, margarine, nutmeg, ground cloves and cinnamon. Stir. Turn burner on to medium heat and cook mixture until heated — 3-5 minutes. Stir once more and serve.

Nathan's Quick Cinnamon Rolls

Nathan Harris   College Station, Texas

Ingredients

1 (7.5-ounce) can refrigerator biscuits
5 teaspoons margarine, softened
10 tablespoons brown sugar
1/2 teaspoon cinnamon
2/3 cup powdered sugar
1 teaspoon water
1/4 cup flour

Equipment

waxed paper
2 small bowls
rolling pin
pastry brush
cookie sheet
measuring cups
small mixing spoon
measuring spoons
wire cooling rack
oven mitts

Preheat oven to 375 degrees.

Open biscuit can carefully following directions on can. Separate biscuits on a large piece of floured, waxed paper placed on the counter top. Flatten each biscuit evenly to 1/8-inch thickness with rolling pin. Next, with pastry brush, spread each biscuit with 1/2 teaspoon margarine. In small bowl, combine brown sugar and cinnamon. Sprinkle each biscuit with 1 tablespoon brown sugar mixture. Roll each biscuit up and place on ungreased cookie sheet. Bake at 375 degrees for 10 minutes until biscuits are golden brown. Carefully re-move cookie sheet from oven using oven mitts and place on cooling rack.

Prepare icing while rolls are cooling. In other bowl, mix powdered sugar and water until mixture is smooth enough to drizzle over the rolls. Let rolls stand 10 minutes. Serve warm.

Cheese and Ham Omlette

Ann Hebert   Crowley, Louisiana

Ingredients

2 large eggs
1/4 cup milk
1 tablespoon onions, diced
1/4 cup ham, cubed
1/4 cup Cheddar cheese, shredded
1 tablespoon margarine
Salt and pepper

Equipment

measuring cups
cutting board
knife
medium mixing bowl
fork
medium skillet with lid
spatula

In bowl, beat eggs and milk with fork until well blended. Add onions, ham, and Cheddar cheese. Place skillet on range burner on medium heat. When skillet is heated, add margarine and melt. Pour egg mixture into skillet. Cover with lid and cook for about 10 minutes or until eggs are set. Remove from heat. Cut omelette in half. Remove with spatula and serve on plate.

Lunch

Ham and Cheese Nibbles

Travis Sawyer Elizabeth City, North Carolina

Ingredients

1 3/4 cups biscuit mix
1 1/2 cups extra sharp Cheddar cheese, grated
2 (4 1/2-ounce) cans deviled ham

Equipment

measuring cups
medium mixing bowl
mixing spoon
cookie sheet
grater
wire cooling rack
oven mitts
serving platter
can opener

Preheat oven to 375 degrees.

To mixing bowl, add biscuit mix, grated cheese and deviled ham. Stir to blend all ingredients well. Roll into 1-inch-size balls. Place balls on ungreased cookie sheet and bake at 375 degrees for 8-10 minutes or until golden brown. Carefully remove cookie sheet from oven with oven mitts and place on cooling rack. Let cool 5 minutes before placing on serving platter. Serve warm.

Rice Balls

Scylla Visperas Lake Jackson, Texas

Ingredients

1 bag Success® Rice
1 small onion, chopped
4 large eggs
2 cups stuffing mix
1½ cups Parmesan cheese, grated
¼ teaspoon garlic powder
½ teaspoon salt
½ teaspoon oregano
¼ cup margarine

Equipment

mixing spoon
fork
small mixing bowl
large mixing bowl
cookie sheet
wire cooling rack
oven mitts
1-quart saucepan
cutting board
knife
measuring cups
measuring spoons
serving platter
grater

Cook rice according to package directions. Preheat oven to 350 degrees. Chop onion with knife on cutting board and set aside. Crack eggs into small mixing bowl and beat with fork. Set aside.

In large bowl, add cooked rice, stuffing mix, onion, cheese, eggs, garlic powder, salt and oregano. Stir ingredients until blended well.

Put margarine into saucepan and heat on range

burner. Set on low heat just until melted — about 1 minute. Pour over rice mixture and stir to blend. Let cool and form rice mixture into 1-inch-size balls and place on ungreased cookie sheet.

Bake at 350 degrees for 15-20 minutes or until golden brown. Carefully remove cookie sheet from oven using oven mitts and place cookie sheet on cooling rack. Let cool for 10 minutes. Arrange on serving platter and serve warm.

Rice Cheddar Melts

Jill R. Perry Winter Springs, Florida

Ingredients	**Equipment**
1 bag Success® Rice	12-inch covered frying pan
1 large egg	large mixing bowl
2 tablespoons flour	fork
1/2 teaspoon baking powder	mixing spoon
1/4 cup milk	wooden spatula
1-2 tablespoons margarine	measuring spoons
1 cup Cheddar cheese, shredded	measuring cups
1/4 cup bacon bits	serving platter
Seasoning salt	

Cook rice according to package directions. Crack egg into bowl and beat with fork. Add cooked rice, flour, baking powder and milk. Stir mixture until well-blended. Put frying pan on range burner and melt margarine over medium heat. Drop rice mixture into pan in tablespoon-sized patties. Cook for 2-3 minutes or until golden brown on one side before turning with spatula. Top browned side of each patty with 1 teaspoon shredded cheese and 1/4 teaspoon bacon bits until cheese and bacon are completely used. Sprinkle with seasoning salt if desired. Cover frying pan and continue to cook until cheese is melted — 2-3 minutes. Remove patties from pan to serving platter. Serve.

PREP TIME
10 min.

Kidiwitches

Greg White   Mulino, Oregon

Ingredients

½ cup Cheddar cheese, grated
⅓ cup sour cream
2 tablespoons peanuts or walnuts, chopped
½ cup carrots, grated
2 tablespoons raisins
3-4 tablespoons butter or margarine, softened
3 slices white bread
3 slices whole wheat bread

Equipment

medium mixing bowl
measuring cups
measuring spoons
butter knife
cutting knife
mixing spoon

Combine Cheddar cheese, sour cream, peanuts or walnuts, carrots, and raisins in bowl, mixing well. Spread butter or margarine on bread. Spread mixture on 3 slices white bread, then top with slices of whole wheat bread. Cut into triangles and serve.

Mexican Manicotti

Christi Hoogestraat Hockessin, Delaware

Ingredients

10 hot dogs
1/2 cup water, boiling
2 (15-ounce) cans chili with beans
1 cup mild taco sauce
10 manicotti shells, uncooked
1/2 cup Monterey Jack cheese, shredded
1/2 cup Cheddar cheese, shredded

Equipment

1-quart saucepan
can opener
measuring cups
12 x 18-inch baking dish
grater
medium mixing bowl
mixing spoon
wire cooling rack
oven mitts
aluminum foil

Preheat oven to 350 degrees. Place 1 hot dog in each manicotti shell and put in ungreased baking dish. Carefully pour boiling water around the sides of dish. In bowl, mix chili and taco sauce together. Pour mixture over hot dogs and pasta. Sprinkle shredded cheeses over the top. Cover tightly with foil.

Bake at 350 degrees for 1 hour or until cheese and sauce are bubbly. Carefully remove dish from oven using oven mitts and place on cooling rack. Let stand 10 minutes before serving.

Easy Cheesy Rice

Jeffrey R. Lind Houston, Texas

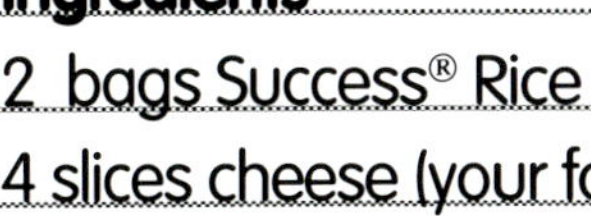

Ingredients

2 bags Success® Rice
4 slices cheese (your favorite!)

Equipment

1-quart saucepan
4 microwave-safe bowls
mixing spoon
microwave oven
measuring cup

Cook rice according to package directions.

Divide rice evenly among microwave-safe bowls. Top each bowl of rice with a slice of cheese. Place each bowl in microwave and cook on high for 30 seconds. Stir, let cool for 2 minutes — then dig in!

Pizza Rice

Scylla Visperas   Lake Jackson, Texas

Ingredients

1 bag Success® Rice
1 large green pepper, chopped
2 tablespoons margarine
1/2 teaspoon garlic powder
1 1/2 cups water
1 (8 1/4-ounce) can whole tomatoes
1 envelope Good Seasons® Italian Salad Dressing mix
1 cup Mozzarella cheese, shredded
1 tablespoon Parmesan cheese, grated
1/2 cup ripe olives, sliced

Equipment

3-quart saucepan
10-inch covered frying pan
cutting board
wooden spoon
knife
grater
measuring cups
measuring spoons
can opener

Cook rice according to package directions.

Chop green pepper into small pieces on cutting board, being careful to remove all seeds. Put saucepan on range burner and add margarine. Heat on medium to high heat until melted. Next, add chopped pepper and garlic powder. Stir pepper and garlic until mixture is tender — about 3 minutes. With heat on medium, add water and tomatoes, breaking tomatoes with spoon into chunks. Stir in salad dressing mix, cover and let mixture come to a full boil for another 3 minutes.

Stir in cooked rice, 3/4 cup shredded Mozzarella cheese and sliced olives. Blend well for 1 minute. Cover and remove from heat. Let stand for 5 minutes and sprinkle with remaining Mozzarella cheese and grated Parmesan cheese. Serve warm.

Yankee Doodle Mac and Cheese

Jennifer Morten   Katy, Texas

Ingredients

1 (8-ounce) package elbow macaroni
2 tablespoons butter
1¼ cups sharp Cheddar cheese, shredded
½ teaspoon salt
Non-stick vegetable oil spray
2 large eggs
3 cups milk
Paprika for garnish

Equipment

2-quart saucepan
1½-quart baking dish
measuring cups
measuring spoons
small mixing bowl
fork
large mixing bowl
mixing spoon
colander
wire cooling rack
oven mitts

Preheat oven to 350 degrees.

Prepare macaroni as directed on package. Place colander in sink, and carefully pour macaroni in, draining thoroughly. Pour drained macaroni into large bowl, adding butter, cheese and salt; toss until butter is melted.

Spray baking dish with non-stick spray. Pour macaroni mixture into dish. In small bowl, beat eggs and milk together with fork. Pour egg mixture over macaroni and sprinkle top with paprika for color.

Bake at 350 degrees in oven 40-50 minutes until cheese is melted and mixture is bubbly. Carefully remove dish from oven with oven mitts and place on cooling rack. Let stand 5 minutes before serving. Serve hot.

Tuna Casserole

PREP TIME 15 min.

COOKING TIME 45 min.

SERVINGS 6

Andrea Karpel Dunwoody, Georgia

Ingredients

- Non-stick vegetable oil spray
- 1 (12-ounce) package egg noodles
- 1 ($10^3/_4$-ounce) can cream of chicken soup
- 3 ($6^1/_8$-ounce) cans of tuna
- Cheddar cheese, grated (optional)

Equipment

- 1-quart saucepan
- 8 x 12-inch oven-proof pan
- strainer
- can opener
- mixing spoon
- oven mitts
- fork
- grater
- wire cooling rack

Preheat oven to 350 degrees. Spray oven-proof pan with non-stick spray and set aside.

Cook noodles according to package directions. Using the strainer, drain noodles in the sink. Spread noodles in pan. Drain tuna and separate into small chunks with fork. Spread tuna over noodles. Then spread cream of chicken soup evenly over noodle and tuna mixture. Top with grated Cheddar cheese, if desired.

Cook at 350 degrees in oven (uncovered) for 35 to 45 minutes, until hot and bubbly. Carefully remove pan from oven with oven mitts and place on cooling rack. Let stand for 5 minutes before serving.

Jamie's Dad's Best Rice

Jamie Pasterczyk   Yonkers, New York

Ingredients

1 bag Success® Rice
Non-stick vegetable oil spray
4 cups prepared tomato sauce
8 ounces Mozzarella cheese, shredded
1/8 cup Romano cheese, grated
1/2 cup Mozzarella cheese, shredded (reserved)

Equipment

medium mixing bowl
mixing cups
2-quart baking dish
wire cooling rack
oven mitts

Cook rice according to package directions. Preheat oven to 350 degrees.

Spray baking dish with non-stick spray. Set aside. In bowl, blend cooked rice, tomato sauce, Mozzarella and Romano cheeses — being sure to reserve 1/2 cup of Mozzarella cheese. Stir mixture to blend, put mixture in baking dish, and top with reserved 1/2 cup Mozzarella cheese.

Bake at 350 degrees in oven for 20-30 minutes until cheese is melted and top is golden brown and bubbly. Using oven mitts, carefully remove baking dish from oven and place on cooling rack. Let stand 5 minutes before serving.

Pepperoni Bread

Amy Andrews Monaca, Pennsylvania

Ingredients
1 (16-ounce) roll of frozen bread dough
1 tablespoon flour
½ pound cheese (your favorite), sliced
1 tablespoon margarine
4 ounces pepperoni, sliced

Equipment
rolling pin
cutting board (or working counter top)
cutting knife
cookie sheet
measuring spoons
oven mitts

Thaw frozen bread dough. (This generally takes several hours.) Dough is ready to work with when it is completely thawed and soft.

When dough is thawed, preheat oven to 350 degrees or temperature listed on frozen bread dough package. Next, prepare your workspace for rolling the dough by sprinkling flour on cutting board or counter top. Spread dough with rolling pin until it makes a rectangular shape and is approximately ½-inch thick. Next, place cheese and pepperoni slices over top of dough. With your hands, roll dough back into original loaf shape. Pinch ends together so melted cheese doesn't escape. Grease cookie sheet with margarine and place loaf on cookie sheet. Bake for 20 minutes or according to frozen bread dough directions. Carefully remove sheet from oven with oven mitts. Slice and serve warm.

Luscious Lunch Pizza Burgers

Crystal Brookes Gales Creek, Oregon

Ingredients	**Equipment**
1 pound lean ground beef	medium mixing bowl
1 (8 ounce) can tomato sauce	wooden spoon
3 tablespoons dried parsley	waxed paper
2 tablespoons dried onion	cookie sheet
1 1/2 teaspoons oregano	measuring spoons
1/2 teaspoon basil	can opener
1 tomato, sliced into 6 slices	oven mitts
1/2 cup Cheddar cheese, shredded	spatula

In a mixing bowl, combine ground beef, tomato sauce, parsley, onion, oregano, and basil. With spoon, mix until all ingredients are combined. Divide mixture into 6 equal portions and place on waxed paper. Form into patties. Place on cookie sheet. Put one slice of tomato on each patty and sprinkle with cheese.

Bake at 375 degrees for 20 minutes. With oven mitts, remove carefully from oven. Place patties with spatula onto a serving platter.

Dinner

Corn Casserole

Trisha Silver   Hackberry, Louisiana

Ingredients

1 bag Success® Rice
1 stick margarine, melted
1 (10¾-ounce) can cream of celery soup
1 (11-ounce) can whole kernel corn with peppers
1 cup sharp Cheddar cheese, shredded

Equipment

medium mixing bowl
2-quart oven-proof casserole dish
mixing spoon
measuring cups
wire cooling rack
oven mitts
can opener

Cook rice according to package directions. Preheat oven to 350 degrees.

In a bowl, combine rice, margarine, soup and corn. Stir to blend. Pour mixture into casserole dish and smooth in an even layer. Sprinkle top with shredded cheese. Bake in 350 degree oven for 20-25 minutes until bubbly. Using oven mitts, carefully remove casserole dish and place on cooling rack. Let stand 5 minutes before serving.

My Fancy Dancy Rice

Ashley McMahan Tucker, Georgia

Ingredients	**Equipment**
1 bag Success® Rice	knife
1 apple	cutting board
1/2 cup walnuts	apple corer
1 cup golden raisins	vegetable peeler
3 tablespoons margarine, softened	measuring cups
2 tablespoons brown sugar	measuring spoons
2 tablespoons light soy sauce	large mixing bowl
2 tablespoons rice vinegar	small mixing bowl
1/2 teaspoon garlic salt	mixing spoon
1/4 cup vegetable oil	wire whisk
2 teaspoons sugar	
1 teaspoon hot mustard	

Cook rice according to package directions. Core apples with apple corer and remove skin with vegetable peeler. Cut apples into 1/4-inch cubes with knife on cutting board. Set aside. Next, chop walnuts on cutting board. Set aside.

To large mixing bowl, add cooked rice, golden raisins, chopped apple, walnuts, margarine and brown sugar. Stir to blend all ingredients well.

In small bowl, combine soy sauce, rice vinegar, garlic salt, oil, sugar and hot mustard. Whisk to blend thoroughly. Pour dressing over rice mixture and toss to coat salad ingredients thoroughly. Serve chilled.

Easy Chicken and Dumplings

David Steele Tuscaloosa, Alabama

PREP TIME 10 min.

Ingredients

2 (14½-ounce) cans chicken broth
1 (6 ¾-ounce) can cooked chicken
10 flour tortillas

Equipment

2-quart saucepan
mixing spoon
knife
cutting board
can opener
fork

Pour chicken broth into saucepan. Break up chicken into smaller pieces with fork and add to broth. Stir to blend.

Place saucepan on range burner and bring to a boil over medium-high heat — about 3 minutes, stirring occasionally. Cut up tortillas into small wedges with knife on cutting board. Add cut-up tortillas to saucepan and stir to blend. Continue to cook until tortillas are tender — about 5 minutes. Serve.

Success-ful Pork Chops

Clint Fullam Kennesaw, Georgia

Ingredients	**Equipment**
1 bag Success® Rice	12-inch frying pan
6 lean pork chops	small mixing bowl
1 (10¾-ounce) can cream of mushroom soup	tongs
1 soup can of water	fork
2 teaspoons poultry seasoning	measuring spoons
¼ teaspoon white pepper	9 x 13 x 2-inch baking pan
Non-stick vegetable spray	ladle
	can opener
	aluminum foil
	oven mitts
	wire cooling rack

Cook rice according to package directions. Preheat oven to 350 degrees.

Preheat frying pan on range burner over medium-high heat. Then add pork chops **carefully** with tongs and let cook until first side is browned — about 3 minutes. When browned, turn pork chops over with tongs and brown on other side — about 2 minutes. If pork chops start to burn, lower heat to medium and continue cooking. When both sides are browned, remove pan from heat. Set aside.

In mixing bowl, add mushroom soup, 1 full soup can of water, poultry seasoning and pepper. Stir to blend.

Spray baking pan with non-stick spray and add cooked rice. Ladle 1 cup of soup mixture over cooked rice and stir to moisten. Smooth rice in an even layer and lay browned pork chops on top of rice — try not to overlap chops. Ladle rest of soup evenly over the pork chops, covering completely. Cover pan tightly with foil and bake in 350 degree oven for 30 minutes or until mixture is bubbly.

Using oven mitts, carefully remove pan from oven and place on cooling rack. **Slowly** remove foil being careful of the hot steam escaping. Let stand 5 minutes before serving.

Easy Texas Red Beans + Rice

Elana Rose Lesartre Houston, Texas

Ingredients

2 bags Success® Rice
2 tablespoons vegetable oil
2 medium onions, sliced
1 (15-ounce) can New Orleans style red kidney beans
1/4 cup canned beef stock or water
1/2 teaspoon salt
1/4 teaspoon pepper

Equipment

measuring cups
mixing spoon
can opener
large mixing bowl
12-inch frying pan
knife
cutting board
can opener
measuring spoons

Cook rice according to package directions. Slice onions with knife on cutting board. Set aside.

Put frying pan on range burner and turn on heat to medium. Add oil and heat 1 minute, then add onions. Cook until lightly browned — about 5 minutes. Next, add undrained beans. Rinse can with beef stock or water and add to beans. Stir to blend. Cook until bean mixture is heated through — about 5 minutes. Add cooked rice, salt and pepper and stir to blend with beans. Cook 5 minutes, stirring occasionally, until heated through and flavors are blended. Serve.

Menu suggestion: Great with beef barbecue.

One-Bowl Meal

Michele Anderson   Minneapolis, Minnesota

Ingredients

2 bags Success® Rice
1 cup cooked meat-chicken, ham, or hot dogs
1 cup Cheddar cheese, shredded
1 cup cooked green peas

Equipment

large mixing bowl
mixing spoon
microwave-proof dish
knife
cutting board
measuring cups
oven mitts
4 serving bowls

Cook rice according to package directions. Cut up meat into half-inch cubes with knife on cutting board. Set aside.

Put cooked rice into mixing bowl and add cheese, meat pieces and peas. Stir to mix well. Pour mixture into microwave-proof dish and smooth into an even layer with spoon. Put dish in microwave and heat on high 1 minute. Stir mixture and heat 30 seconds longer or until heated through. Using oven mitts, carefully remove dish from microwave. Stir again and divide equally into 4 serving bowls. Serve.

South-Of-The-Border Rice

Pam Simmons San Antonio, Texas

Ingredients	**Equipment**
1 bag Success® Rice	1-quart saucepan
8 ounces sour cream	mixing spoon
1 (1¼-ounce) packet taco seasoning mix	measuring spoons
½ cup Cheddar cheese, shredded	measuring cups
2 green onions, chopped	1½-quart casserole dish
1 large tomato, diced	wire cooling rack
¼ cup black olives, sliced (optional)	oven mitts
Jalapeno pepper slices (optional)	knife
	cutting board

Cook rice according to package directions. Preheat oven to 350 degrees.

While rice cooks, spoon sour cream into saucepan and place on range burner on low heat. When sour cream begins to gently bubble — in about 1 minute — add taco seasoning, **1 teaspoon at a time**, stirring well after each addition. (Continue adding taco seasoning to taste. You may not want to use the whole package.) When taco seasoning has been added, cook 4 more minutes, then remove from range and set aside. Next, chop green onions and dice tomato with knife on cutting board. Set aside.

Put cooked rice in casserole dish and stir in cooked sour cream mixture. Top with shredded cheese. Bake in 350 degree oven for 20 minutes until cheese is melted and mixture is heated through. Using oven mitts, carefully remove casserole from oven and place on cooling rack. Top with green onions, tomato, black olives and jalapeno pepper (optional). Let stand 5 minutes before serving.

Hot Dog Pizza

Maranda Prior Sacramento, California

Ingredients

1 box pizza crust mix
4 hot dogs
1 (14-ounce) jar prepared pizza sauce
1 cup Cheddar cheese, shredded

Equipment

12-inch round pizza pan or cookie sheet
knife
cutting board
mixing spoon
measuring cups
wire cooling rack
oven mitts

Preheat oven to 375 degrees.

Prepare pizza crust mix as directed on package. Spoon pizza sauce on top of crust and spread evenly. Slice hot dogs 1/4-inch thick with knife on cutting board. Arrange sliced hot dogs on crust as desired — you can make designs! Sprinkle shredded cheese on top.

Bake in 375 degree oven for 20 minutes or until cheese is melted and bubbly. Using oven mitts, carefully remove pizza from oven and place on cooling rack. Let stand 5 minutes before cutting into wedges. Serve hot.

Honey-Roasted Brown Rice

Jacob Thiessen Pollock Pines, California

Ingredients

1 bag Success® Brown Rice
2 tablespoons butter
1 cup honey-roasted peanuts

Equipment

10-inch frying pan
measuring cups
measuring spoons
wooden spatula
serving bowl

Cook rice according to package directions.

Place frying pan on range burner and let butter melt over medium heat. Add peanuts as soon as butter is melted. Cook peanuts for 5 minutes stirring occasionally with the wooden spatula. Next, add cooked brown rice to nuts in pan, stirring to blend. Cook 5 more minutes over low heat until heated through.

Carefully pour out rice/nut mixture into serving bowl and serve.

Tiffany's Yummy Rice

Tiffany Smith Lake Jackson, Texas

Ingredients	**Equipment**
1 bag Success® Rice	10-inch frying pan
1 pound ground beef	serving bowl
1/4 cup onion, chopped	knife
1/4 teaspoon sugar	cutting board
1/4 cup Italian salad dressing	measuring cups
1 teaspoon margarine, melted	measuring spoons
1 (8-ounce) can tomato sauce	medium mixing bowl
Water	mixing spoon
	can opener

Cook rice according to package directions. Place frying pan on range burner and add ground beef. Cook over medium heat until all traces of pink are gone — about 3 minutes. Break up chunks of meat with spoon. Remove pan from burner and drain excess liquid from pan. Set pan aside. Next, chop onion with knife on cutting board and add to drained ground beef. To the same pan, add sugar, cooked rice, salad dressing, margarine and tomato sauce. Stir until all ingredients are blended. Add water as needed to adjust consistency.

Return pan to burner and set on medium heat and cook until mixture bubbles and is heated through –about 4 minutes. Pour into serving bowl and serve immediately. Store leftover rice in refrigerator in airtight container.

Cheesie Chicken Casserole

Brian Pangarakis Bronson, Texas

Ingredients

2 bags Success® Rice
2 cups chicken, cooked, removed from bone and cubed
1 (10¾-ounce) can cream of broccoli soup
1 cup Cheddar cheese, shredded

Equipment

medium mixing bowl
2-quart microwave-proof dish
mixing spoon
measuring cups
oven mitts
can opener

Cook rice according to package directions. In mixing bowl, combine rice, chicken, soup and cheese and stir.

Pour mixture into microwave-proof dish and smooth to an even layer. Put dish in microwave oven and cook on high for 5-7 minutes or until cheese is melted and bubbly. Using oven mitts, carefully remove dish from oven and serve.

Grandmother's Porcupine Balls

Samantha Lee Borrow/Stern **Seattle, Washington**

Ingredients

1 bag Success® Rice
1 1/4 pounds hamburger
1 (10 3/4 -ounce) can tomato soup
1/4 soup can water
1 tablespoon onion powder
Pinch salt and pepper

Equipments

2-quart covered saucepan
wooden spoon
measuring cups
measuring spoons
mixing spoon
can opener
knife
cutting board

Cook rice according to package directions. Let cool.

Combine ground beef and cooked rice and mix well. Shape into small meatballs. Set aside.

Pour tomato soup, water and onion powder into saucepan. Add salt and pepper. Stir well. Heat slowly on range burner on medium heat for 10 minutes.

Drop meatballs into heated sauce and cover pan. Simmer on low to medium heat for 15 minutes. Stir once gently. Serve hot.

Luke's Fiesta Rice Salad

PREP TIME 15 min.

Luke McNeil   Rogers, Arkansas

Ingredients

1 bag Success® Rice
2 cups chicken, cooked and chopped
½ cup raisins
¼ cup celery, finely diced
2 tablespoons sunflower seeds
1 cup prepared creamy bacon or Ranch salad dressing
1 (11-ounce) can Mandarin orange segments
4 large red-leaf lettuce leaves, for garnish

Equipment

large mixing bowl
measuring spoons
mixing spoon
measuring cups
can opener
knife
cutting board
strainer
4 small serving bowls
plastic wrap
paper towels

Cook rice according to package directions. In large mixing bowl, combine rice, chicken, raisins, celery, and sunflower seeds. Next, add your choice of prepared salad dressing and stir to coat all ingredients well with dressing. Pour orange segments into strainer and let drain well. Carefully fold orange segments into mixture, being careful not to mash them. Cover tightly with plastic wrap and chill in the refrigerator for at least 1 hour.

To serve: Wash lettuce leaves and dry thoroughly on paper towels. Line small serving bowls with cleaned and dried lettuce leaves and spoon chilled salad into the center of each dish. Serve chilled.

Fun Tortillas

Jeffrey Hodges   Lake Jackson, Texas

Ingredients

1 bag Success® Rice
1 pound lean ground beef or ground turkey
½ teaspoon salt, optional
¼ teaspoon pepper, optional
1 (1¼-ounce) envelope taco seasoning mix
10 tortillas
8 ounces mild picante sauce
2 cups Cheddar or Monterey Jack cheese, shredded

Equipment

10-inch frying pan
wooden spoon
measuring cups
measuring spoons

Cook rice according to package directions. Place frying pan on range burner, add ground meat and turn heat setting on medium-high heat. Cook meat until all traces of pink are gone, breaking up chunks of meat with spoon. Cook about 3 minutes and drain excess juices from pan. If desired, season with salt and pepper. Add taco seasoning, stirring to blend well. Fill tortillas with equal amounts of meat mixture, cooked rice, picante sauce and cheese. Fold over sides of tortillas. Serve.

Spanish Rice

Cristel Johnson Bee Branch, Arkansas

Ingredients

1 bag Success® Rice
1/2 pound hamburger, browned
1 (10 3/4-ounce) can vegetable beef soup
1/2 soup can water
1 tablespoon onion flakes
1 teaspoon paprika
1 teaspoon chili powder
1/4 teaspoon seasoned salt
1/2 cup ketchup
2 tablespoons mild salsa
1/2 teaspoon pepper

Equipment

large mixing bowl
measuring cups
mixing spoon
3-quart saucepan
can opener
measuring spoons
frying pan

Cook rice according to package directions. Place frying pan on range burner and turn heat setting on medium-high heat. Cook meat until all traces of pink are gone, breaking up chunks of meat with spoon. Cook about 3 minutes and drain excess juices from pan. Add other ingredients in order listed and stir. Set on low heat. Simmer mixture until hot and bubbly — about 20 minutes, stirring occasionally. Serve.

Brandi's Chicken

Brandi Taylor Pinehurst, Texas

Ingredients

2 bags Success® Rice
1 tablespoon margarine
1/4 cup green pepper, chopped
1/4 cup celery, chopped
1/4 cup onion, chopped
2 (10 3/4-ounce) cans cream of mushroom soup
1/4 cup milk
8 ounces cream cheese, cubed
1 (1-ounce) packet Ranch dressing mix
Non-stick vegetable oil spray
1 (2 1/2-pound) chicken, cut into 8 pieces

Equipment

9 x 13 x 2-inch baking pan
can opener
knife
cutting board
measuring cups
measuring spoons
10-inch frying pan
aluminum foil
oven mitts
wire cooling rack

Cook rice according to package directions. Preheat oven to 350 degrees.

Place frying pan on range burner and turn heat to medium-high. Add margarine and melt. Add pepper, celery and onion. Cook until onions and celery are clear or about 5 minutes. Lower heat to medium and add soup, milk, cream cheese and dressing mix. Blend and heat for 2-3 minutes. Spray baking dish with non-stick spray and layer bottom with chicken pieces. Pour soup mixture over chicken and spread evenly. Cover pan tightly with foil and bake in 350 degree oven for 1 hour. Using oven mitts, carefully remove dish from oven and place on cooling rack. Let stand 5 minutes. Serve over hot cooked Success® Rice.

Morgan's Chili Chip Pie

Morgan Dailey Beckville, Texas

Ingredients	**Equipment**
½ cup chopped onion	1-quart casserole dish
3 cups corn chips	knife
1 (15-ounce) can chili	cutting board
1 cup Cheddar cheese, shredded	wire cooling rack
¼ cup sliced black olives	oven mitts
Sour cream (optional)	measuring cups
Taco sauce (optional)	can opener

Preheat oven to 375 degrees.

Chop onion with knife on cutting board. Set aside.

Layer 2 cups of corn chips into ungreased casserole dish. Add chili and spread evenly over chips. Sprinkle onion, cheese, and sliced black olives over chip/chili mixture. Top with remaining cup of corn chips.

Bake in 375 degree oven for about 20 minutes or until mixture is bubbly. Using oven mitts, carefully remove casserole dish from oven and place on wire cooling rack. Let stand for 5 minutes before serving. Serve hot and garnish with sour cream or taco sauce, if desired.

Rice + Chicken Bake

Diana Humphries El Cajon, California

Ingredients

1 bag Success® Rice
2 cups chicken, cooked and chopped
1 (10¾-ounce) can cream of chicken soup
1 tablespoon chopped pimiento
1 (16-ounce) can cut green beans

Equipment

large mixing bowl
mixing spoon
2-quart casserole dish
fork
wire cooling rack
oven mitts
strainer
can opener

Cook rice according to package directions. Preheat oven to 325 degrees.

In bowl, break up cooked chicken into smaller chunks with fork. Next add soup, cooked rice and pimiento. Stir until all ingredients are well blended. Pour contents of can of green beans into strainer to drain. Add drained green beans to bowl and gently stir to blend. Pour into ungreased casserole dish and bake in 325 degree oven for 40 minutes or until firm.

Using oven mitts, carefully remove casserole dish from oven and place on cooling rack. Let stand for 5 minutes before serving.

Chicken Goolash

Lamar Swink Duluth, Georgia

Ingredients	**Equipment**
2 bags Success® Rice	can opener
1 (6 3/4-ounce) can chunk chicken	fork
1 cup milk	2-quart covered saucepan
1 (10 3/4-ounce) can cream of chicken soup	mixing spoon
1 cup water	3 serving plates
	measuring cups

Cook rice according to package directions. Break up chicken into smaller chunks with a fork. Put chicken, milk, soup and water into saucepan. Stir to blend.

Place pan on range burner and turn heat to medium. Cover pan and bring to a boil, stirring occasionally — about 3 minutes. Continue to cook another 3 minutes until heated through.

Place cooked rice on 3 plates. Spoon chicken soup mixture over cooked rice and serve.

Broccoli + Rice

Renee Nichols   Fair Grove, Missouri

Ingredients	**Equipment**
1 bag Success® Rice	can opener
1 (10-ounce) box frozen broccoli spears, thawed	2-quart saucepan
1 ($10^3/_4$-ounce) can cream of mushroom soup	measuring cups
3 tablespoons margarine	measuring spoons
1 (8-ounce) jar pasteurized processed cheese spread	mixing bowl
1 tablespoon dried onion flakes	2-quart casserole dish
	wire cooling rack
	oven mitts

Cook rice according to package directions. Preheat oven to 350 degrees.

Add broccoli, soup, margarine, cheese spread, dried onion flakes and rice to saucepan. Stir to blend. Place saucepan on range burner, turn burner to medium-heat and cook until heated through — about 3 minutes, stirring occasionally.

Pour heated mixture into ungreased casserole dish and spread out evenly. Bake in 350 degree oven for 30 minutes or until bubbly. Using oven mitts, carefully remove from oven and place on cooling rack. Let stand 5 minutes before serving.

Franks and Beans Olé

Justin Michael Kane   Wantagen, New York

Ingredients	**Equipment**
2 (20 ounce) cans red kidney beans	can opener
2 (8 ounce) cans tomato sauce	medium saucepan
3 tablespoons brown sugar	knife
8 hot dogs, sliced	measuring spoons
¼ teaspoon dry ground mustard	measuring cup
4 long slices American cheese	4 serving bowls
2 cups corn chips	

In saucepan, combine beans, tomato sauce, brown sugar, dry mustard and hot dog slices. Heat on range burner at medium heat for 10 minutes. Stir occasionally. While beans-hot dog mixture is heating, put ½ cup of corn chips in each individual serving bowl. Add 1 cup hot beans-hot dog mixture over corn chips in each bowl. Place a slice of cheese on top of each serving.

Snacks and
Desserts

A Bit-Of-Honey Shake

Ben Nichols Fair Grove, Missouri

Ingredients	**Equipment**
4 big scoops vanilla ice cream	blender
1 cup milk	ice cream scoop
1 tablespoon peanut butter	measuring cups
1 teaspoon vanilla	measuring spoons
1 tablespoon honey	drinking glasses

Put ice cream into blender and add milk, peanut butter, vanilla and honey. Blend on high speed until thick and smooth. Pour into 1 large glass or 2 small glasses and serve immediately.

Sweet Potato Applesauce

Meagan Christina Worth-Cappell Newark, Ohio

Ingredients

2 large apples
1/2 cup water
1 large sweet potato
1 cup apple juice
4 tablespoons honey
1/2 teaspoon cinnamon

Equipment

apple corer
vegetable peeler
knife
2-quart saucepan with cover
cutting board
1-quart saucepan
strainer
electric blender
mixing bowl
measuring cups
measuring spoons
cutting board

Core apples with apple corer and peel with vegetable peeler. Cut apples into 1/2-inch cubes with knife on cutting board. Put apple cubes in 2-quart saucepan and add water. Cover and put on range burner; set on medium-heat and cook until water comes to a boil and apple chunks are soft — about 5 minutes. Drain and set aside.

Peel sweet potato with vegetable peeler and cut into 1-inch chunks with knife on cutting board. Put chunks into 1-quart saucepan and cover with water. Put pan on range burner and set on medium-high heat. Bring to a boil and cook until potatoes are soft, about 5 minutes. When potato chunks are done, remove from range and pour into strainer over the sink to drain. Put sweet potatoes into blender. Cover and blend on high for 1 minute or until smooth, adding cooked apples, apple juice, honey, and cinnamon. Serve warm.

Raspberry Cranberry Salad

Sierra Jones Wilmington, Delaware

Ingredients

1½ cups water
1 (3-ounce box) raspberry gelatin*
1 (3-ounce box) lemon gelatin*
1 (10-ounce) box frozen raspberries
1 (16-ounce) can cranberry raspberry jellied sauce
1 cup of lemon/lime soda
½ cup sliced almonds
*Can use sugar-free gelatin, if desired.

Equipment

1-quart covered saucepan
large mixing bowl
mixing spoon
fork
measuring cups
plastic wrap

Pour water into saucepan and put on range burner. Cover and bring to a boil over high heat– about 2 minutes.

Put raspberry and lemon gelatins in bowl. Pour boiling water over gelatin and stir to dissolve. Next, stir in frozen raspberries, breaking up clumps with spoon. Stir cranberry/raspberry sauce with fork to loosen up. Add sauce to gelatin mixture and stir to blend all ingredients well. Chill until partially set — 30 minutes. When gelatin is partially set, carefully pour in lemon/lime soda while stirring gently. Cover with plastic wrap and chill 5-6 hours or overnight. When gelatin is set, sprinkle top with sliced almonds and serve.

Puppy Chow

Tara Brown   Oldtown, Maryland

Ingredients	**Equipment**
1 stick margarine	2-quart saucepan
½ cup peanut butter	mixing spoon
1 cup chocolate chips	measuring cups
6 cups Rice Chex® cereal	large mixing bowl
2 cups powdered sugar	large paper bag

Put margarine, peanut butter and chocolate chips in saucepan and place on range burner. Turn on heat to low and stir with spoon continuously until melted. Pour melted mixture into mixing bowl and stir in cereal until well coated.

Put powdered sugar in paper bag and add coated cereal. Close bag tightly and shake vigorously until cereal separates into bite-size clumps. Store in an airtight container.

Easy Pineapple Cream Pie

Deborah Eck Enid, Oklahoma

Ingredients

2 (8-inch) pie shells
1 (20-ounce) can crushed pineapple, undrained
1 (14-ounce) can sweetened condensed milk
1 tablespoon lemon juice
1 cup pecans, chopped
1 (16-ounce) tub non-dairy whipped topping

Equipment

fork
cookie sheet
oven mitts
wire cooling rack
large mixing bowl
measuring cups
mixing spoon
measuring spoons
rubber spatula
knife
can opener
chopping board

Preheat oven to 400 degrees. Prick thawed pie with the tines of fork. Place on cookie sheet and bake in 400 degree oven for 8-10 minutes or until golden in color. Using oven mitts, carefully remove cookie sheet from oven and place on cooling rack. While shells cool, prepare filling. In bowl, combine pineapple, condensed milk, lemon juice and nuts. Blend. Add whipped topping and blend . Divide filling evenly between **cooled** shells and smooth evenly with spatula. Place in refrigerator and cool completely — about 3 hours. Serve chilled.

Yum-Yum Cubes

Renee Nichols Fair Grove, Missouri

Ingredients

1 (5-ounce) package of your favorite flavored, sugar-sweetened soft drink mix

Water as directed on package

Equipment

2-quart pitcher

2 ice cube trays

mixing spoon

24 wooden sticks

Prepare sugar-sweetened soft drink mix according to package directions. Pour into clean ice cube trays and put in freezer, making sure that tray lays flat. Insert wooden stick when partially frozen. Leave in freezer until frozen solid.

Pineapple Surprise

Michael Day   Gilmanton, New Hampshire

Ingredients

Non-stick vegetable oil spray
3 tablespoons flour
1 (18¼-ounce) box yellow cake mix
1 (3⅛-ounce) box instant vanilla pudding mix
1 cup milk
1 (16-ounce) tub whipped topping
8 ounces cream cheese, softened
1 (20-ounce) can crushed pineapple, drained
1 cup coconut flakes (optional)
½ cup walnuts, chopped
8 Maraschino cherries, cut in half

Equipment

2 large mixing bowls
electric mixer
10 x 15 inch jelly roll cake pan
2 wire cooling racks
oven mitts
measuring cups
wire whisk
mixing spoon
rubber spatula
medium mixing bowl
can opener
tongs

Preheat oven to 350 degrees.

Spray jelly roll pan with non-stick spray, sprinkle with flour, turning pan to coat evenly. Discard loose flour.

Prepare cake in mixing bowl with electric mixer according to package directions. Spread mixture in jelly roll pan and bake at 350 degrees in oven for 30-35 minutes.

Using oven mitts, carefully remove cake from oven and place on cooling rack. Carefully place other cooling rack over the top of cake and turn pan over to unmold cake. Allow to cool completely — about 1 hour.

To prepare frosting: Put pudding mix in a bowl, add milk and stir to blend. Set aside. In another bowl, beat whipped topping and cream cheese with whisk until fluffy. Add pudding mixture and stir to blend. Add pineapple and blend. Turn cooled cake over onto serving plate and spread frosting on top and sides of cake with spatula, covering completely and evenly. Next, sprinkle with walnuts, cherries, and coconut (if desired).

Cover cake carefully with plastic wrap — don't mash icing. Refrigerate until frosting is set — about 2 hours. Serve chilled and keep refrigerated.

Caramel Rolls

John Peterson Blaine, Minnesota

Ingredients	**Equipment**
Non-stick vegetable oil spray	9 x 13 x 2-inch cake pan
2 (16-ounce) loaves frozen bread dough	2-quart saucepan
1 stick margarine, softened	mixing spoon
1 teaspoon vanilla extract	oven mitts
1 cup brown sugar	measuring cups
1 (3⅝-ounce) box butterscotch cook-and-serve pudding mix	measuring spoons
½ cup chopped nuts (optional)	wire cooling rack
	knife

Spray cake pan with non-stick spray. Place bread dough in cake pan and let sit and rise at room temperature for 2 hours. Divide thawed dough into 12 pieces. Roll each piece into a baseball-sized ball and spread in pan. Set aside. Preheat oven to 350 degrees. In saucepan, mix margarine, vanilla, brown sugar, and pudding mix. Heat on medium heat until the margarine melts. Stir to blend into a smooth mixture, adding nuts, if desired.

Carefully pour mixture over the rolls. Let the rolls rise one more time until they double in size — about 1 hour.

Bake rolls at 350 degrees for 30 minutes. Using oven mitts, carefully remove pan from oven and place on cooling rack. Cool for 5 minutes before cutting. Serve warm.

Colada Coolers

Emily Wells   Fengus Falls, Minnesota

Ingredients

1 small banana
1 (8-ounce) container vanilla yogurt
1 teaspoon coconut or vanilla extract
½ cup pineapple juice
2 tablespoons sunflower seeds (optional)

Equipment

medium mixing bowl
fork
mixing spoon
measuring cups
measuring spoons
6 (3-ounce) paper cups
6 wooden sticks (optional)

Mash banana in bowl with fork. Add yogurt, vanilla, juice and sunflower seeds. Stir. Pour into paper cups. Freeze until firm. Inserl wooden sticks when coolers are partially frozen — after about 2 hours. To serve, tear away paper cup and eat on a stick or put in a bowl and eat with a spoon.

Yummy Treats

Megan Kirby Flint, Michigan

Ingredients

1 (18½ ounce) box white cake mix
3 cups coconut flakes
Red food coloring
2 large eggs
½ cup vegetable oil

Equipment

small, medium, and large mixing bowls
measuring cups
cookie sheet
mixing spoon
2 forks
oven mitts
wire cooling rack
serving platter

Preheat oven to 350 degrees. Empty cake mix into large mixing bowl. Set aside. Put coconut in medium bowl. Add red food coloring, a few drops at a time, stirring well with fork after each addition until you get an even red color. Set aside.

Beat eggs in small bowl with other fork. Add eggs to cake mix alternately with vegetable oil, stirring well after each addition. Roll mixture into small balls about 1-inch in size. Roll balls in colored coconut to coat completely. Place coconut-covered balls on an ungreased cookie sheet and bake at 350 degrees in oven for 8-10 minutes. Do not overbake. Using oven mitts, carefully remove cookie sheet from oven and place on cooling rack. Let stand for 5 minutes and remove treats to serving platter. Serve. Store leftover treats in an airtight container.

Pizza Dip

Jonathan Nebe Houston, Texas

Ingredients

3 green onions, chopped
8 ounces cream cheese, softened
1 cup pizza sauce
8 ounces Mozzarella cheese, shredded
1/2 teaspoon dried basil
1/2 teaspoon dried oregano
Tortilla chips or crackers for dipping

Equipment

measuring cups
measuring spoons
small mixing bowl
fork
rubber spatula
8 x 8 x 12-inch glass baking dish
knife
cutting board
oven mitts
wire cooling rack

Preheat oven to 350 degrees. Chop green onions with a knife on a cutting board. Set aside.

Put cream cheese in small bowl and beat with fork until fluffy. Spread in an even layer in an ungreased baking dish. Spread pizza sauce evenly over cream cheese. Top evenly with cheese and green onions. Sprinkle top completely with basil and oregano.

Bake at 350 degrees in oven for 30 minutes until cheese is melted and top is light golden brown. Using oven mitts, carefully remove baking dish from oven and place on cooling rack. Let stand 5 minutes before serving. To serve: Dip tortilla chips or crackers into dip and enjoy!

Sweet Success

Rachel Autenrieth Lake Jackson, Texas

Ingredients	**Equipment**
1 bag Success® Brown Rice	small microwave-proof dish
1/4 cup heavy cream or milk	measuring cups
1/4 teaspoon cinnamon	measuring spoons
1 tablespoon margarine	mixing spoon
1/4 cup coconut, shredded	oven mitts
2 teaspoons brown sugar	

Cook rice according to package directions.

In microwave-proof dish, add cooked brown rice, cream or milk, cinnamon, margarine, coconut, and brown sugar. Stir to blend. Place dish in microwave oven and heat on high for 2-4 minutes or until heated thoroughly. Using oven mitts, carefully remove dish from oven and place on cooling rack. Stir mixture once more and serve.

Delicious Instant Rice Pudding

Jeffrey Schrank Norcross, Georgia

Ingredients	**Equipment**
1 bag Success® Rice	measuring cups
2 large eggs	measuring spoons
2 cups milk	fork
1/2 teaspoon vanilla extract	medium mixing bowl
1/4 teaspoon cinnamon	2-quart saucepan
1/8 teaspoon nutmeg	plastic wrap
1/2 cup sugar	mixing spoons
1/4 cup raisins	
1/2 cup mini-marshmallows (optional)	

Cook rice according to package directions.

Crack eggs in bowl and beat with a fork. Set aside. In saucepan, stir to blend rice, milk, vanilla, cinnamon, nutmeg, sugar, and raisins. Put saucepan on range burner and heat on medium until mixture comes to a gentle boil — about 3 minutes, stirring constantly. Reduce heat to low and continue to cook until raisins are plump — about 5 minutes. Stir occasionally. Remove pan from heat. **Carefully** pour hot rice mixture into beaten eggs — a little at a time — stirring well after each addition so that eggs will not "scramble." Keep adding rice mixture and stirring well until all liquid is added to eggs. Cool mixture for 10 minutes at room temperature. Garnish with mini-marshmallows, if desired.

Waldorf Salad

Terry Milien Orlando, Florida

Ingredients	**Equipment**
2 cups Granny Smith apples	medium mixing bowl
1 teaspoon lemon juice	small mixing bowl
½ cup walnuts or almonds, chopped	knife
1 cup celery, chopped	cutting board
½ cup raisins	mixing spoon
¼ cup mayonnaise	vegetable peeler
½ cup whipped topping	apple corer
¼ cup coconut flakes	plastic wrap
	measuring cups
	measuring spoons

Core apple with apple corer and remove skin with vegetable peeler. Chop apple into ½-inch cubes with knife on cutting board. Put apple cubes into medium bowl and pour lemon juice over the apple cubes. Toss apple cubes to coat well with juice. Chop nuts and celery on cutting board. Add both to apple cubes. Add raisins.

In small bowl, combine mayonnaise, whipped topping and coconut flakes. Stir to blend well. Add dressing to apple mixture and toss to coat all ingredients thoroughly.

Cover tightly with plastic wrap and put in refrigerator to chill for at least 1 hour. Serve chilled.

Pink Passion

Charity Brown   Oldtown, Maryland

Ingredients	Equipment
1 (20-ounce) can cherry pie filling	large mixing bowl
1 (12-ounce) tub whipped topping	mixing spoon
1 (15 1/2-ounce) can crushed pineapple	rubber spatula
	measuring cup
1 cup nuts (optional)	plastic wrap
1 (14-ounce) can sweetened condensed milk	can opener
	knife
1 cup shredded coconut (optional)	chopping board

Combine all ingredients in bowl and blend well. Cover tightly with plastic wrap and put in refrigerator until completely chilled — at least 3 hours. Serve chilled.

Chocolate Crunchy Snacks

Loren Dietz   Marietta, Georgia

Ingredients

1 cup butterscotch chips
3/4 cup milk chocolate chips
1/4 cup mint or semi-sweet chocolate chips
1/2 cup peanut butter
6 cups toasted rice cereal

Equipment

double boiler (or 10-inch frying pan plus 2-quart saucepan)
9 x 13 x 2-inch baking pan
mixing spoon
rubber spatula
large mixing bowl
knife
measuring cups

If you do not have a double boiler, you can make one by putting butterscotch and chocolate chips in a 2-quart saucepan then placing the saucepan in a 10-inch frying pan. Put both pans on range burner. Pour enough hot water into the frying pan so that saucepan sits in about 2 inches of water. Turn on burner to medium-high setting until water starts to bubble and butterscotch/chocolate mixture is melted — about 3-5 minutes. Stir to blend. Remove saucepan from hot water, blend in peanut butter. Set aside.

Put cereal in mixing bowl and pour chocolate/peanut butter mixture over cereal. Stir gently to coat cereal thoroughly. Scrape contents out of bowl into cake pan with spatula, smoothing to make an even layer. Cool until hardened or about 30 minutes. Cut hardened mixture with knife into twelve 3-inch squares. Store leftover crunchies in refrigerator in an airtight container.

Mixed Fruit Whip

Jenny Smethers   Pensacola, Florida

Ingredients	**Equipment**
1 cup fruit cocktail	can opener
1 cup Mandarin orange segments	large mixing bowl
½ cup mixed nuts, chopped	mixing spoon
1 cup raisins	cutting board, knife
1 (8-ounce) tub whipped topping	strainer
	plastic wrap
	measuring cups

Drain fruit cocktail and Mandarin oranges in a strainer. Set aside.

Chop nuts with knife on cutting board. Set aside.

To bowl, add nuts, raisins, oranges, and fruit cocktail. Add whipped topping. Stir gently to coat all ingredients well with whipped topping. Cover bowl tightly with plastic wrap. Put in refrigerator until thoroughly chilled — at least 3 hours. Serve chilled.

SERVINGS
36

Peanut Butter Bars and Frosting

Ryan Tapper Plymouth, Minnesota

Ingredients	**Equipment**
1/2 cup + 2 tablespoons margarine	2 medium mixing bowls
1 cup peanut butter	mixing spoon
1 1/4 cups sugar	measuring cups
1/4 cup corn syrup	measuring spoons
1 1/4 teaspoons salt	rubber spatula
1 large egg	10 x 15-inch jelly roll pan
1/4 cup water	wire cooling rack
1 3/4 cup flour	oven mitts
	fork
	metal frosting spatula

FROSTING
2 tablespoons margarine, softened
1 tablespoon peanut butter, softened
1/2 teaspoon vanilla extract
2 tablespoons milk
1 1/2 cups powdered sugar

Preheat oven to 350 degrees.

In bowl, cream margarine and peanut butter together. Add sugar, corn syrup, salt, egg, and water. Mix thoroughly. Mix in flour, being careful not to overmix.

Spread mixture into **ungreased** 10 x 15-inch jelly roll

pan. Bake at 350 degrees for 20-30 minutes until golden brown — do not overbake! Using oven mitts, carefully remove from oven and place on a wire rack to cool. Prepare frosting.

To prepare frosting:

To mixing bowl add margarine, peanut butter, vanilla extract, and milk. Beat with a fork until light and fluffy. Add powdered sugar, a little at a time, blending well after each addition. When all sugar has been added, continue to beat frosting until light and fluffy. Spread prepared frosting in an even layer on **cooled** bars. Cut into 2-inch squares. Store leftover bars in an airtight container.

Serving suggestion: Top bars with your choice of raisins, mini-marshmallows, peanuts, M&Ms® or Reese's Pieces®.

Spiders

Melissa Humphries El Cajon, California

Ingredients
2 cups chocolate chips
Water for double boiler
1 cup corn flakes
1 cup chow mein noodles

Equipment
double boiler (or 2-quart saucepan and 10-inch frying pan)
mixing spoon
waxed paper
serving platter
teaspoon

Melt chocolate chips in a double boiler. If you do not have a double boiler, you can make one by putting chocolate chips in a 2-quart saucepan and then placing the saucepan in a 10-inch frying pan. Put both pans on range burner. Pour enough hot water into the frying pan so that saucepan sits in about 2 inches of water. Turn on burner to medium-high setting and heat until water starts to bubble and chocolate is melted — about 3-5 minutes. Stir melted chocolate to blend. Add corn flakes and mix in gently. Drop by teaspoonfuls onto waxed paper. Stick noodles into the sides of the drop to make the spider legs. Refrigerate about — 15 minutes — transfer to serving platter.

Party Cones

Donovan Schoniger   Keystone, South Dakota

Ingredients

1 cup salted peanuts or mixed nuts
1 cup raisins
1 cup M&Ms®
1 cup Cheerios® or Rice Chex® cereal
6 flat-bottomed ice cream cones

Equipment

large mixing bowl
mixing spoon
measuring cup

In bowl, mix peanuts or mixed nuts, raisins, M&Ms® and cereal. Spoon out mixture into the flat-bottomed ice cream cones to approximately 3/4 full. Place 1 cone at each party guest's place at the table.

Apple-Rice Pizza

Alyssa Miller Iota, Louisiana

Ingredients

CRUST
1 bag Success® Rice
3 large eggs, beaten
1 cup Cheddar cheese, shredded

FILLING
1 bag Success® Rice
1 (3.4-ounce) box vanilla instant pudding
2 cups milk
1 (22-ounce) can apple pie filling

FOR GARNISH
1 cup shredded cheese

Equipment

wire whisk
medium mixing bowl
10-inch deep dish pie plate
oven mitts
2-quart saucepan
mixing spoon
small bowl
fork
wire cooling rack
rubber spatula
measuring cups
can opener

Cook rice according to package directions.

For crust: Preheat oven to 450 degrees. In bowl, beat eggs with whisk. Add cooked rice and cheese. Blend well. Press mixture into pie plate and smooth with the back of a spoon into an even layer on bottom and sides of plate. Bake at 450 degrees for 12 minutes. Using oven mitts,carefully remove plate from oven and place on cooling rack. While crust is cooling, prepare filling.

For filling: Combine pudding and milk in saucepan, stir. Add cooked rice and stir. Put saucepan on range burner and cook over medium heat until mixture comes to a boil, stirring constantly — about 5 minutes. Pour pudding mixture into cooled crust and let stand until mixture is set — about 30 minutes. Spread apple pie filling over the pudding mixture in an even layer with spatula and sprinkle top with cheese. Refrigerate to cool completely — about 3 hours. Serve chilled.

SERVINGS
15

Glorified Rice

Haley Wixson Fisher, Arizona

Ingredients

2 bags Success® Rice
2 large apples
2 tablespoons lemon juice
3/4 cup Maraschino cherries
1 cup mini-marshmallows
1 (8-ounce) can flaked coconut
3/4 cup sugar
1 (15 1/2-ounce) can crushed pineapple, drained
1 (16-ounce) tub whipped topping

Equipment

measuring spoons
measuring cups
large mixing bowl
mixing spoon
rubber spatula
apple corer
small mixing bowl
vegetable peeler
knife, cutting board
plastic wrap
can opener
paper towels

Cook rice according to package directions. Core apples with apple corer and remove skin with vegetable peeler. Chop apples into 1/4-inch cubes with knife on a cutting board. Put apples into small bowl, add lemon juice and toss apples to coat completely so they will not turn brown. Cut Maraschino cherries in half, drain well on paper towels and chop with knife on cutting board. Set aside.

To large mixing bowl, add cooked rice, mini-marshmallows, coconut, cherries, apples, sugar, and pineapple. Stir these ingredients completely. Fold in whipped topping into bowl with spatula. Cover bowl tightly with plastic wrap and refrigerate 1 hour before serving.

After School Snack

Christine Welsh Lock Haven, Pennsylvania

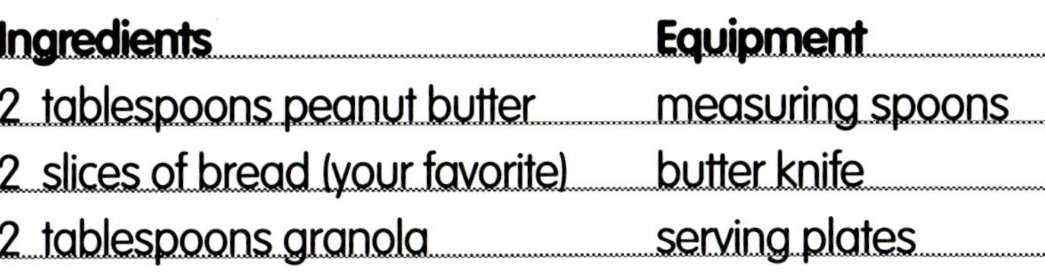

Ingredients	**Equipment**
2 tablespoons peanut butter	measuring spoons
2 slices of bread (your favorite)	butter knife
2 tablespoons granola	serving plates
2 tablespoons chocolate chips	

Spread 1 tablespoon peanut butter on each slice of bread to cover completely. Sprinkle 1 tablespoon granola and 1 tablespoon chocolate chips evenly over the peanut butter layer. Place slices of prepared bread on serving plates and enjoy with an ice cold glass of milk!

Peanut Butter Lootey Fruitey

Erin Kade   Miami, Florida

Ingredients	**Equipment**
½ cup peanut butter	measuring cups
½ cup pineapple, crushed, undrained	medium mixing bowl
¼ cup slivered almonds	butter knife
12 pitted dates	plastic wrap
¼ cup raisins	rubber spatula
4-6 slices bread	food processor
	can opener
	knife

Combine peanut butter, undrained pineapple, almonds, dates and raisins into work bowl of a food processor, cover, and blend for 10 seconds. Turn off processor and scrape down sides of work bowl with spatula. Cover and blend again — about 2 minutes — until mixture is smooth. Remove mixture with a spatula from work bowl into mixing bowl.

Spread mixture on a slice of your favorite type of bread with a butter knife. Cut slice in half with other knife and put one half on top of the other. Wrap sandwich in plastic wrap and pack in your lunch for a yummy treat! Cover remaining mixture in bowl tightly with plastic wrap and store in refrigerator.

Hot Chocolate Mix

Jessica N. Elliot Bedford, Pennsylvania

Ingredients

1 (2-pound) box instant cocoa mix
1 (22-ounce) jar coffee creamer
1 pound box confectioner's sugar
1 (25.6-ounce) box powdered milk
Mini-marshmallows (optional)

Equipment

extra large mixing bowl
mixing spoon
1-gallon plastic container

In bowl, pour cocoa mix, coffee creamer, sugar, and powdered milk. Stir to blend.

To store: Pour mixture and store in an airtight, plastic container.

To serve: Add 4 heaping teaspoons to an 8-ounce cup of boiling water. Garnish with 5-6 mini-marshmallows for an added treat!

Candle Salad

Brandon Depew Womego, Kansas

Ingredients	**Equipment**
4 large lettuce leaves	knife
4 pineapple rings	plates
2 small bananas	small bowl
1/3 cup lemon juice	toothpicks
1/3 cup mayonnaise	butter knife
4 Maraschino cherries	measuring cups

Rinse and dry 4 lettuce leaves. Place pineapple rings individually on each lettuce leaf, then place each leaf on a plate. Peel bananas and cut each one in half. Pour lemon juice in a small bowl. Dip each banana half in juice. Next, spread mayonnaise around the hole of each pineapple slice. Then, take banana halves and stand up in the hole of pineapple slices. Put a dab of mayonnaise on the tip of each banana. Top each banana with a cherry, secured with a toothpick.

Rice Krispie Treats

Amy Pastor Crowley, Louisiana

Ingredients

Non-stick vegetable oil spray
½ cup light or dark corn syrup
1 cup sugar
1 cup creamy or chunky peanut butter
½ cup unsweetened cocoa powder
6 cups Rice Krispies® cereal

Equipment

13 x 9 x 2-inch cake pan
3-quart saucepan
mixing spoon
rubber spatula
measuring cups

Coat cake pan with non-stick spray and set aside. Combine corn syrup, sugar, peanut butter, and cocoa in a saucepan. Put saucepan on range burner and turn on heat to medium and bring to a boil, stirring constantly. Remove from heat. Add cereal and stir to coat cereal completely. Spread mixture into cake pan and smooth mixture with spatula. Let cool about 1 hour and cut into 2-inch squares. Store leftover treats in an airtight container.

Hay Stacks

David Steele Tuscaloosa, Alabama

Ingredients

1 cup salted mixed nuts,chopped
2 (6-ounce) bags butterscotch chips
1 tablespoon vegetable oil
1 (3-ounce) can of chow mein noodles

Equipment

double boiler (or 10-inch frying pan and 2-quart saucepan)
measuring cups
measuring spoons
knife
cutting board
tablespoon
waxed paper

Chop nuts with knife on cutting board. Set aside.

Melt butterscotch chips with vegetable oil in a double boiler. If you do not have one, you can make a double boiler by putting butterscotch chips and vegetable oil in a 2-quart saucepan. Then place the saucepan in a 10-inch frying pan. Put both pans on top of range burner. Pour enough hot water into the frying pan so that saucepan sits in about 2-inches of water. Turn on burner to medium heat setting until water starts to bubble and chips are melted — about 3-5 minutes. Stir melted chips to blend. Remove saucepan from hot water and add salted nuts and chow mein noodles. Stir to coat all ingredients. Drop by tablespoons onto waxed paper. Let stand on waxed paper until set — about 15 minutes. Store leftovers in airtight container.

Shelly Kroeger   Cody, Nebraska

Ingredients

1 (6-ounce) box black cherry flavored gelatin*
3 cups water
1 (21-ounce) can blueberry pie filling
1 (8-ounce) tub whipped topping
*can use sugar-free gelatin if desired

Equipment

1-quart saucepan
measuring cups
can opener
medium mixing bowl
mixing spoon
plastic wrap

Put gelatin in bowl. Set aside. Pour water into saucepan and place on range burner. Bring to a boil over high heat — about 2-3 minutes. Carefully pour hot water over gelatin in bowl and stir with spoon until dissolved. Add blueberry pie filling and stir until well mixed. Cover bowl tightly with plastic wrap and put in refrigerator. Keep in refrigerator until thoroughly chilled and gelatin is set -- about 2 to 3 hours. When set, top with whipped topping and serve.

Recipe idea: You also can use cherry pie filling instead of the blueberry for a Double Cherry Jelly-Belly Salad.

Teenage Party Punch

Natalie Perez Houston, Texas

Ingredients	**Equipment**
3 (1-liter) bottles lemon/lime soda	large mixing bowl
3 (5-ounce) packets strawberry sugar-sweetened soft drink mix	mixing spoon
	measuring cup
3 cups sugar	punch bowl
1 (46-ounce) can pineapple juice	can opener

Put soda bottles in refrigerator to cool until ready to use. In bowl, combine soft drink mix, sugar, and juice. Blend well. Chill mixture thoroughly in refrigerator — at least 3 hours. When ready to serve, pour punch mixture into punch bowl and add chilled soda. Stir to blend. Serve immediately.

No Bake Peach Pie

Danny Shaqareq Jacksonville, Florida

Ingredients

1 (16-ounce) can sliced peaches, reserve juice
1 (16-ounce) box Ritz® or Hi-Ho® crackers

Equipment

9-inch glass pie plate
strainer
small bowl
plastic wrap
can opener

Drain sliced peaches with a strainer over bowl, reserving juice.

In pie plate, line bottom and sides with crackers overlapping them to cover bottom and sides so dish does not show through. Layer crackers with peaches. Repeat layering with crackers and peaches until peaches are used up, ending with a cracker layer on top. There will be crackers leftover. Pour reserved peach juice over top of pie. Cover tightly with plastic wrap and place pie in refrigerator. Let set until thoroughly chilled — at least 3 hours. Serve chilled.

Fresh Carrot-Rice Pudding

William Tanner   Miami, Florida

Ingredients

1 cup Success® Rice
1 (3 1/8-ounce) box cook-and-serve vanilla pudding mix
1/2 teaspoon cinnamon
2 cups milk
1/2 cup raw carrot, shredded
3 tablespoons golden raisins

Equipment

2-quart saucepan
mixing spoons
measuring cups
measuring spoons
large mixing bowl
plastic wrap

Cook rice according to package directions. Pour pudding mix into saucepan and sprinkle in cinnamon. **Slowly** add milk as you stir. Cook over medium-low heat until thick and boiling, stirring constantly. Remove saucepan from heat and stir in carrot, rice, and raisins.

Pour mixture into bowl, cover tightly with plastic wrap and cool thoroughly in the refrigerator — about 3 hours. Serve chilled.

Raggedy Robins

Stephanie Smith Lucama, North Carolina

Ingredients
1 cup sugar
3 teaspoons cocoa powder
1/4 cup margarine
1/4 cup milk
1/2 teaspoon vanilla extract
1 1/2 cups quick-cooking oatmeal
1/4 cup peanut butter

Equipment
1-quart saucepan
measuring cups
measuring spoons
waxed paper
teaspoon
mixing spoon

Put saucepan on range burner and add sugar, cocoa, margarine and milk. Stir to blend. Turn range burner to medium heat. Continue stirring and bring to a boil. Boil for 1 minute.

Remove saucepan from heat and **quickly** stir in vanilla extract, oatmeal, and peanut butter. Make sure all ingredients are well-blended. Working quickly, drop mixture onto waxed paper by the teaspoon. Cool 15 minutes. Store completely cooled Raggedy Robins in an airtight container.

Summer Time Pie

Betsy Reid   Birmingham, Alabama

Ingredients	**Equipment**
1 (6-ounce) can frozen lemonade or limeade, thawed	can opener
1 (14-ounce) can sweetened condensed milk	medium mixing bowl
1 (9-ounce) carton whipped topping, thawed	wooden spoon
1 (8-inch) prepared graham cracker pie shell	knife
Slices of lemon or limes	cutting board

In bowl, mix limeade or lemonade with sweetened condensed milk. Fold in whipped topping. Pour mixture into pie shell and smooth out evenly. Refrigerate until firm—about 2 hours.

Garnish with fresh lime or lemon slices. Place slices of lemons or limes on individual pie slices.

Crafts

No-Scratch Scrubbie Ball

Terry Herzig Glenburn, North Dakota

Supplies

1 needle
nylon thread
2 yards nylon netting in 2 different colors
scissors

Thread the needle with the nylon thread, tying a knot in 1 end. Cut the netting into 4-inch strips. Take 1 strip of each of 2 colors and weave the needle through the center of the strips, using a zig-zag motion. When you have woven the needle through the 2 strips, pull the thread through the netting, gathering it up. Then wrap the thread around the center of the strip a few times and tie it off.

Makes 5 Scrubbies.

Shaker Rhythm Instruments

Alex Crotty Conyers, Georgia

Supplies

self-sticking designer contact paper
1 empty plastic pill box
scissors
2 tablespoons Success® Rice, uncooked
measuring spoons

Cut the self-sticking contact paper into a small piece to cover the outside of the pill box. Fill the pill box with the rice. Cover the cap with contact paper, replace the cap and cover with self-stick paper to seal.

Makes 1 instrument.

Placecards

Ryan White Tigard, Oregon

Supplies

Drawing paper

Colored felt-tip markers or crayons

On pieces of paper — 1 for each guest — write each guest's name and draw a fun picture, making it colorful by using the different colored markers. When the placecards are finished, put cards around the table at the place where each guest will be sitting.

State-Of-The-Art-Rice

Michelle Anderson   Minneapolis, Minnesota

Supplies

4 bags of Success® Rice, uncooked
4 (1/4-ounce) bottles of food coloring, assorted colors
4 small bowls
4 metal spoons
1 pencil
sturdy construction paper
craft glue

Empty 1 bag of rice into each bowl. Next, add bottles of food coloring — a different color for each bowl — stirring with a different spoon for each bowl to coat rice evenly with color. Let rice dry for 5 minutes before using.

While rice is drying, draw a simple, large design on construction paper. Beginning at the top of the picture, spread a thin layer of glue over your design. Then sprinkle the appropriate color of rice on that segment. For example, your picture might be a blue sky, green grass, a yellow sun and a red flower. Each color of rice would be used to "color" the picture. Dry thoroughly before hanging.

Edible Necklace

Danielle McGhan Bottineau, North Dakota

Supplies

1 needle
1 (18-inch) piece of string
Lifesavers® candy
short macaroni, uncooked
colored mini-marshmallows
short licorice pieces

Thread the needle with string. Alternate candy, macaroni, marshmallows and licorice pieces on the string until the necklace is filled. Tie off the ends of string. Now you have an edible necklace!

Makes 1 necklace.

Face Paint

Kerri McGinty Huntington, New York

Supplies

1 teaspoon cornstarch

½ teaspoon water

few drops of food coloring

½ teaspoon cold cream

muffin tin

small paint brush or cotton swab

measuring spoons

small mixing spoon

In muffin tin, mix cornstarch, water, food coloring and cold cream, blending well. Apply to face or arms with small paint brush or cotton swab.

Makes enough to paint 1 face.

Tip: Recipe can be multiplied to make different colors!

Make Your Own Stickers

Donovan Schoniger Keystone, South Dakota

Supplies

assorted color crayons or felt-tip markers
brown parcel tape (the kind that must be moistened on the back)
scissors

Draw and color pretty pictures on the non-stick side of the tape, using lots of colors. Cut out the shapes you have drawn. Moisten the stickers with water and attach them to your notebooks or lunch box. Grandparents love them on letters!

William's Play Dough

William David Steele   Tuscaloosa, Alabama

Supplies
1-quart saucepan
1 cup all-purpose flour
1 cup water
½ cup salt
2 teaspoons cream of tartar
wax paper
measuring cups
measuring spoons

With adult supervision, mix ingredients in saucepan and heat on low heat for 3 minutes. Knead on wax paper. Store in airtight container.

Makes 1 pound of play dough.

Rainbow Ball

Donovan Schoniger   Keystone, South Dakota

Supplies

assorted colored seed beads
straight pins
1 ($^1/_2$-inch-wide) colored ribbon
1 (6-inch) diameter styrofoam ball
scissors

Put the different colored beads on the pins and stick them into the styrofoam ball. Use different color combinations to make them pretty. If you make a mistake, just pull the pins out and start over! Cut ribbon in an 8-inch strand and pin at the top of the ball at the center to make a hanging loop.

Makes 1 ball.

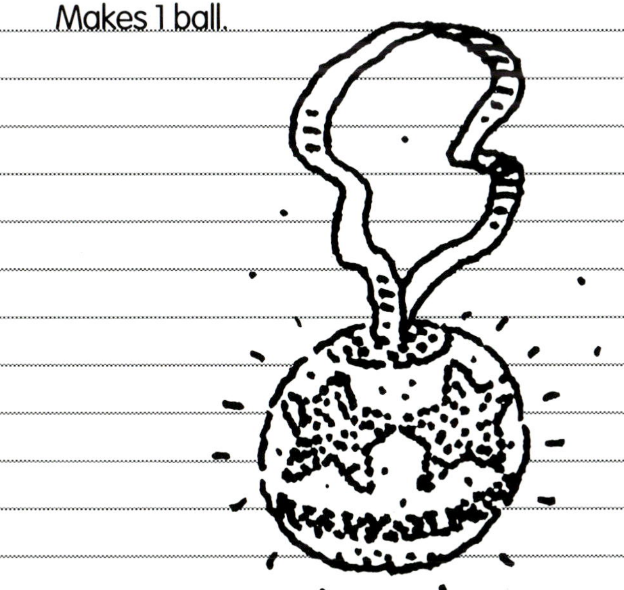

Indian Shield

Mike Slatton   Claremore, Oklahoma

Supplies

1 (12-inch square) piece of cardboard
scissors
assorted color felt-tip markers
embroidery needle
thread
4 jingle bells
3 feathers
1 (11-inch) piece of string
masking tape

Cut a 12-inch circle out of cardboard with scissors. With markers, draw different Indian designs on cardboard. Thread needle and attach bells around the designs. Evenly space feathers at the bottom of the shield, tape the quill end to the back of cardboard, leaving feathers hanging down. Fold string in thirds and tape each end to the back of the shield to make a handle.

Makes 1 shield.

Glossary

Adjust To "adjust seasoning" means that just before serving, food is tasted and the appropriate seasoning is added if needed.

Bake To cook food in an oven by dry heat, set at a specific temperature for a set length of time. It is important to know how accurate your oven is, since many vary in setting — either hotter or cooler than the selected temperature. We recommend using an oven thermometer to check the actual temperature inside the oven.

Bake Blind Method of baking a pie crust before it is filled. Method: Using the tines of a fork, poke the bottom and sides of the pastry-lined pie plate all over. This will keep the crust from bubbling up during baking and becoming uneven. Then place a sheet of aluminum foil or parchment paper on top of crust and smooth gently. Next, pour in dried beans (Navy or Pinto work well) or uncooked rice to use as weights. Bake in preheated oven. Remove the foil/paper and weights to bake uncovered for the last 5 minutes until crust is an even golden brown.

Batter Uncooked liquid mixture for cakes, muffins, pancakes, crepes or waffles. Main ingredients are usually flour, eggs and milk. Also can be used to coat various foods before they are fried.

Blend To mix 2 or more ingredients together with a spoon or electric mixer or blender until combined.

Boil In recipes "bring to boil" means the process of heating liquids in a pan on a range burner, usually on high heat until bubbles break the surface. It also means to cook food in boiling liquid. The term "a full rolling boil" results when bubbles continue even when stirring.

Boil-in-Bag On range, lower bag into 1 quart of boiling water in saucepan. Boil uncovered for 10 minutes. In micro-wave, lower bag into 2 cups of water in 1½ quart micro-wave-safe dish. Cover and cook on high for 10 minutes. Remove bag from dish or saucepan and drain.

Broil To cook food directly under or above an intense heat source. This can be done in an oven or on an indoor or outdoor grill.

Brown To cook food very quickly on high heat on the range burner or in the oven until surface is "browned" while center of food remains moist.

Chop To cut food into smaller pieces. Chopped food gives you larger pieces than minced food.

Combine To mix 2 or more ingredients together so that they are mixed and no longer separated.

Core To remove the core from a fruit — such as an apple.

Cream To beat 1 or more ingredients until soft, smooth and creamy.

Crumble To break food up with fingers — such as bread or bacon — into small pieces.

Cube To cut food into squares in the size dictated by the recipe — such as $\frac{1}{2}$ inch.

Dash A very small amount of seasoning added to food in a quick downward hand action. A dash is equal to about 5 drops or $\frac{1}{10}$ ounce.

Dice To cut food into tiny cubes from $\frac{1}{8}$ to $\frac{1}{4}$ inch in size.

Dissolve To blend a dry ingredient (such as sugar, salt, flour, gelatin or yeast) into a liquid until no trace of grains can be seen or felt.

Double Boiler A set of 2 pans in which a smaller one fits into the large, leaving a few inches which is filled with water until it touches the bottom of the smaller pan. The small pan has a cover. Double boilers are used to heat or melt delicate ingredients such as custards or chocolate.

Drain To pour off the liquid or grease from food such as canned food or cooked meat. It can also mean to blot fried foods with paper towels to remove excess grease.

Fold A blending movement used to gently combine a light, fluffy mixture such as whipped cream or beaten egg whites into a heavier mixture such as mousse or pudding. The lighter mixture is added in 1/4 amounts and is cut through the other mixture vertically with a rubber spatula in a circular motion. The bowl is rotated 1/4 turn in the opposite direction from the cutting motion. This process should continue until the light mixture has been completely blended into the other.

Frost To cover a cooked cake completely with frosting or icing.

Garnish To decorate a dish with appropriate fruits or vegetables such as cherries or olives to make the dish look more appetizing.

Grate To cut food — such as cheese or carrots — into thin pieces by drawing it across a utensil called a grater. Food that has been grated is easier to blend with other foods or is used as topping.

Grease & Flour To rub a pan with vegetable oil or margarine and then coat with flour. This helps prevent food from sticking to the pan.

Melt The process of heating a food — such as margarine, cheese or chocolate — slowly over low heat until it becomes liquid.

Mince To cut food with a knife into very small pieces. Pieces are smaller in size than chopped food.

Peel To remove the skin of a fruit or vegetable such as an apple or potato with a small knife or vegetable peeler utensil.

Prick See Bake Blind

Seasoning Ingredients such as herbs, spices and condiments added to foods to add flavor.

Seed To remove seeds from fruits or vegetables.

Simmer Boil gently on low heat.

Whip To beat ingredients such as cream or egg whites until light and fluffy. The beating incorporates air into the mixture thereby making it light and fluffy.

Index